THE ART OF COACHING

HOW TO EXPLAIN CLEARLY AND BECOME A GOOD LEADER AND COACH

BY SMART READS

I0478372

Free Audiobook

As a thank you for being a Smart Reader you can choose 2 FREE audiobooks from audible.com. Simply sign up for free by visiting www.audibletrial.com/Travis to get your books.

Visit:
www.smartreads.co/freebooks
to receive Smart Reads books for FREE

Check us out on Instagram:
www.instagram.com/smart_readers
@smart_readers

ABOUT SMARTREADS

Choose Smart Reads and get smart every time. Smart Reads sorts through all the best content and condenses the most helpful information into easily digestible chunks.

We design our books to be short, easy to read and highly informative. Leaving you with maximum understanding in the least amount of time.

Smart Reads aims to accelerate the spread of quality information so we've taken the copyright off everything we publish and donate our material directly to the public domain. You can read our uncopyright below.

We believe in paying it forward and donate 5% of our net sales to Pencils of Promise to build schools, train teachers and support child education.

To limit our footprint and restore forests around the globe we are planting a tree for every 10 hardcover books we sell.

Thanks for choosing Smart Reads and helping us help the planet.

Sincerely,

Travis & the Smart Reads Team

TABLE OF CONTENTS

INTRODUCTION

Coaching is not only useful; it is necessary. A team is only as good as its leader as the old adage goes. The success of a team is measured by the success of her or his leader, just as the effectiveness of a leader is in direct proportion to the effectiveness of the team. Both are mutually dependent.

Many managers, CEOs, community leaders, politicians, business leaders, etc., are equipped with all the technical skills, training, savvy and knowledge pertinent to their fields. Yet often they lack the means to engage their colleagues and workers to share their goals and enthusiasm. This is what coaching is all about. It is not enough to receive reports and respond to them. A good leader needs to be able to inspire, to unlock the creative potential in others, and this what many, many professional training programs do not do.

This book will serve as an introduction to the art of coaching. You'll be taught a number of principles that can be applied in any leadership situation and in any professional role, whether it be entrepreneur, manager, leader of a community outreach group, church leader, coach of the school football team or leader of any other enterprise where you are called upon to be a role model and inspiration.

Coaching doesn't require degrees in psychology or counseling, but it does require the cultivation of certain qualities – respectfulness, trustworthiness, commitment, the ability to see the positive and honesty. Anybody who see coaching as the art of passing on one's own wisdom and is not willing to be disavowed of that notion should really stop reading now. If you decide to be a coach it will be a challenging yet life-changing venture not just for your future clients, but for you as well. The qualities listed above are the qualities of a great human being, and that is what you will be striving to become.

CHAPTER 1: WHAT IS COACHING?

Coach – v. to train (somebody) intensively by instruction, demonstration and practice. *(Source: The Penguin Concise Dictionary)*

In years past, students would often hire tutors to help them prepare for their exams, as indeed, many still do. These tutors were likened to horse-drawn carriages, or coaches, in that they carried their charges down the academic road to their desired destination. And so the word came to mean any person who was a mentor.

Many people will have negative memories of being "coached." Perhaps they were shouted at by their school baseball coach, belittled by the gym instructor, or badgered by a teacher to do better. These experiences do not represent what coaching is. Note the three elements of coaching: instruction, demonstration and practice. There is nothing about shouting or belittling. In fact, such an abuse of authority demonstrates a failure in leadership.

The element of instruction in coaching should be minimal. Demonstration and practice will play the dominant part. Good educators will tell you instruction, though it plays its part, is the least effective method of teaching. By itself it is useless in the long term. Yet this is how so many people are educated.

Coaching, like any good teaching, is not centered on authority - "I teach. You learn." That is not to say that good coaching is not founded on personal authority. It most certainly is, but that authority comes from personal commitment, enthusiasm, experience and confidence. It is the kind of authority all of us can respect. Nearly everyone knows or has known people in their lives who have exuded that kind of authority. It might be a parent who has helped them through a personal crisis. It might be an employer who mentored them when they began a job. It might be an older sibling or a friend who kept encouraging them to succeed and made them believe they could succeed. These relationships did not make people dependent upon their mentors, but rather, encouraged independence. They realized how they could bring their own unique insights and talents to the enterprise they were undertaking. A good coach does not seek to be emulated, but rather wants the student to discover his or her own potential.

If more educators realized what teaching should be all about there would be a lot more happy, creative and self-reliant people in the world.

There are four fundamental principles of good coaching. They are trust, unlocking potential, commitment and effective implementation of goals.

CHAPTER 2: ESTABLISHING TRUST

Trust is, of course, the basis of any effective relationship, and this certainly holds for a coaching relationship. Coaching involves the sharing of goals, ideals and resources. Both mentor and disciple risk being vulnerable to each other, because there is a certain intimacy in the relationship that goes beyond being merely acquaintances. How can the disciple expose his mind and heart to you if he does not trust you? For the relationship to work, trust is essential.

So what does trust look like in a coaching relationship? There are three components people can identify.

Interest – Having an authentic concern for a person. You will want the individual you are hoping to coach to succeed. You will be interested in their goals, their plans for the future. You will want to discover more about them, to learn about their talents and ideas. You will want them to open up to you with confidence and without fear (see integrity and confidentiality below).

It happens that employers do not show a genuine interest in their employees because they see in them potential competition. They fear that they will take knowledge, expertise and professional secrets from the company, leave and establish themselves in competition. Of course this happens. Yet by showing no interest or enthusiasm for your gifted and talented employees you are more likely to make this happen. But if you invest genuine time, concern and curiosity in them isn't it more likely that they will want to hang around?

Integrity – This means your integrity. You must not only appear to be a person worthy of trust, but actually are one. Personal authority does not guarantee any degree of personal integrity and everyone knows that. In fact, being in authority may work against you. People are naturally suspicious of authority. In fact, the higher the authority, the greater the suspicion of unethical behavior. Most know the famous words of Lord Acton (1834 – 1902), writing to Bishop Mandell Creighton, "Power tends to corrupt, and absolute power corrupts absolutely." He went on to write "Great men are almost always bad men...There is no worse heresy than that the office sanctifies the holder of it."

Prejudice – An often justified prejudice that you are fighting against. Becoming the exception to the rule in the eyes of your employees may be difficult and it will take time. Honor and protect their conditions of employment. Model the very behavior you expect to see in them. So if they are expected to clock in at 9:00 A.M., you will be there at 8:50. If their lunch break is half an hour, so is yours.

Confidentiality – How many of us have had the experience of not going to an employer with a problem for fear it will be used against us in the workplace? For instance, it's not unusual for workers who underreport accidents in the workplace. The reason they were under – reported was the fear that these accidents would reflect badly on employees. They believed they might be disciplined or even sacked when in fact it was the employer's responsibility to maintain a safe workplace. Yet if they felt as if they could approach their employer without trepidation how much safer the workplace might have become! A good coach will encourage persons to come to him or her in confidence and keep that confidence. If someone gives you a great idea in confidence, don't steal it. Invite that person to work on it with you, and give them the credit. If an employee approaches you with a personal problem, don't blab about it, and certainly don't use it to modify or terminate their terms of employment.

It's all about authenticity. You cannot fake interest. You cannot pretend to be a person of integrity. Confidentiality cannot be simulated. You may get away with it for a short time, but you will always be found out. In establishing trust, which is fundamental to any fruitful relationship, let alone a coaching one, you must work at it hard and you must work at it consistently. Trust is easy to lose but hard to gain and even harder to regain once lost. And if you're sitting in the boss's chair you are, simply by that fact, at a considerable handicap.

CHAPTER 3: UNLOCKING POTENTIAL

Coaching is centered on one individual. There isn't a method of mass coaching. Organizations often hire so – called coaches to address conferences or to conduct retreats and workshops, but all these can do is impart general information that the individual must appropriate and adapt to their specific needs. Yet if they don't know what their needs are, these gatherings have little merit for them. This is the job of a personal coach.

Everyone's vision for themselves will be different, and there is no "one size fits all" approach. The coach must eliminate preconceptions about goal setting. The aim is not to mold carbon copies of him. That will never happen. Individuals who try to achieve goals often fail because they pursue goals that are not theirs; they are those of someone else, and they believe their success lies in emulating the achievements of another person. Yet how will you be successful, if, wanting to go to Florida, you are instead on the road to Nevada?

So how do you help an individual identify their goals? First, get to know the individual. Talk to them and ask them about their lives. Listen to their stories, and when they are talking, listen. By that, listen to their concerns, their interests, their desires, their dreams, their ideals. You will begin to create a picture of who this person is. What motivates him or her? What drives him or her? What makes them tick? Where is she going? How does he see his world? Personal, professional and academic records can only tell you so much. He may have become top of his class in college, but why? She is in the engineering industry but her records show she excelled in customer relations. What's that all about? George in Accounting often goes off hiking in the wilderness. What does that tell me about him?

You will also gain an idea of the kinds of obstacles your employees are facing in their careers and in their private lives. What disappointments and failures, perceived or real, do they labor under?

When listening to your employees, don't simply listen to what they say. Active listening also entails observing body language, behaviors and tone. Does he or she avoid eye contact? Does she fold her arms when you talk to her? Touching the nose when saying something – what does that mean? Do certain words or phrases act as emotional triggers? Why does he seem to tense up when you mention a certain topic. Non – verbal gestures can generally tell you more about a person than what they actually say.

It is important to remind yourself about the importance of confidentiality. It's crucial not disclose personal information about your employees except with their permission and for serious reasons. It is only ethical to do so without their permission if there is a serious reason, such as to prevent a crime or serious harm to a third person. To violate this confidentiality would be a breach of trust, and in many countries and jurisdictions, it is illegal and might be seen as criminal action.

It's important for our coaching clients to be open, and to feel safe. Make them trust you. Now trust is a two way street. So if you prize openness, you must be open as well. You must be prepared to speak from the heart and disclose your thoughts, feelings, desires, disappointments and failures. Just as your employee has made himself or herself vulnerable, so too must you. This takes courage, as well as prudence. But the best way to disarm somebody and make them feel safe is to disarm yourself. In days of yore when two knights, strangers to each other, met, they shook hands. This was more than a symbol, for the hand they shook with (usually the right hand) was also the hand that held a sword. So to shake hands was to disarm oneself. And so when you coach, you must disarm yourself of your own swords, that is, the authority that creates distance between employer and employee.

Of course there are boundaries that have to be observed. The relationship of employer to employee still needs to be respected. If you find an employee is violating your confidentiality or otherwise overstepping boundaries, they may need a gentle reminder. But by and large, you will find that the respect you have for your employees will be generously returned.

CHAPTER 4: CHALLENGING THOUGHT PATTERNS

Each person behaves according to a certain point of view. People have ideas about themselves and the world, which establish patterns of thought. These patterns dictate beliefs and behavior. For example, someone may approach every project from the point of view of practicality. '"Is this practical? "they will ask. Others will have a more idealistic approach. "Let's do this!" they will say. Many, sadly, have a negative opinion of themselves and will not attempt any project. The ideas that move behaviors come from education, experience and temperament. Some may be positive while others not so.

Some of these beliefs can be traced to specific events. Traumatic events in the person's life, such as childhood abuse, can have a deep and lasting effect on people's personalities.

A good coach will be able to identify these beliefs, encourage the positive ones and challenge the negative.

How can you make a person think differently, especially when they have been thinking in a certain way for many years, perhaps even a lifetime? Well, you can't. The individual must take a conscious choice to change their way of thinking and make positive choices. However the coach can help a person to reflect on how they think and how that impacts their lives. A good mentor can help the individual to identify pivotal moments in their lives and re-assess them.

Take this example, there was a fellow who was a good writer – a very good writer. This man's dream was in fact to earn his living as a writer. But he didn't have the courage to do it. Instead he went from job to job. He was a teacher, a tour guide, a childcare worker, a disability worker, even a minister of religion at one time. Yet he never stayed in one occupation for very long. He remained unsatisfied. In the end he didn't even write very much.

With coaching, he was able to identify a deep-seated lack of confidence. He didn't want to succeed, because it was somehow easier and safer to fail. As a child he had been clumsy – often breaking things, and a little vague. He was always forgetting things and getting the wrong end of the stick. He wasn't simple, but sometimes he didn't quite understand what was going on around him. The negative reaction that he often received deeply affected him, making him believe he really was incapable of success.

Then someone asked him to ghostwrite a book. He was reluctant at first. It was a big job. He didn't think he could do it, but with encouragement he gave it a go, and mentored him through it. He finished it, to his client's great delight. Now he has given up his job and is writing in the attic of his house all day. He's making money. And he's happy.

A good coach encourages people to identify and draw upon the strengths they already have and use these to empower themselves. A good coach does not offer false hope or dismiss real challenges. The coach and his client deal in what is true. There is no need to invent anything. If Suzie thinks she has a poor head for figures, and she actually does, putting her in the accounting department will not help.

Notice that this approach takes time – a long time. Try to get out of the habit of thinking of your employees as resources. You are investing your time and interest in them as individuals. Each individual is different, and will move at his or her own pace. Often they will stall. Often they will go backwards. You will need to be patient. And because you are dealing with individuals, do not expect the result that you want to happen right away or in the manner you imagined. Rather, encourage your client to discover his or her own power, and then see how that power can benefit your organization. A coach cannot tailor individuals to his own needs. After all, a coach does not create anything. He simply allows an individual to blossom.

Another word of caution, and an important one. In the course of this process you may very well uncover some dark places. You may deal with individuals marked by trauma – childhood abuse, violence, grief, guilt, etc. You may unwittingly open up wounds. You may witness disturbing behaviors such as self-harm or violence. If this happens recognize that your client may need professional assistance. Do not charge in where angels fear to tread. Seek help if you are unsure of what to do. It is your duty of care as a coach.

CHAPTER 5: COMMITMENT

Your client has recognized the belief patterns that direct how he or she thinks and acts. They have identified what they really want out of life and how their thoughts are an obstacle to achieving what their desires. It is one thing to bring a horse to water, as the saying goes, but another to make it drink.

Actually that adage is not entirely apt, because you don't want to make your client choose anything. You want to encourage her to make the decision herself and commit to it. Without commitment nothing will change. She has to take ownership of her own destiny. So how do you motivate your clients to embrace life-changing decisions?

The first thing to accomplish is to have your client formulate a vision of who they want to be and what they want to accomplish. That vision must be their own – not yours. That vision must be achievable. Setting an unrealistic goal only sets oneself up for failure, and then they may lose faith in themselves and in your role as a coach. The goals should be as specific as possible and should be divided into steps. It is much easier, less daunting, and safer, to go up a ladder rung by rung rather than by jumping.

Suppose someone is an engineer, but his real passion is health. Let's say he wants to be a health consultant – a dietician. He needs to establish a time frame, say five years. Before that he will need to do a number of things; gain the relevant training, learn to manage a business, hook – up with a mentor, adjust his finances, perhaps freelance for a while and at the same time continuing in his present occupation, etc. The coach and employee can plan the steps necessary to achieve his ultimate goal, becoming a dietician.

But what can your future dietician do now, in his present role, to start the process? A great way to motivate is to identify something than can be done immediately to get the ball rolling. Perhaps he could advise employees as an unofficial consultant. Perhaps he could be in charge of a good – eating program in the workplace.

It is important to identify benchmarks of success for each goal. He then has something specific to indicate when he has succeeded. If he undertakes the good – eating program he may decide he needs to target every department of the organization within, say six weeks. When studying he might set himself the benchmark of studying twenty hours a week. These benchmarks should, of course, be realistic and achievable. Moreover, there should be flexibility in the plan. Some goals may be reached faster or slower than others. The goal posts will then change, and the plan is then adapted.

Remember that each goal should be practical. It must be achievable. Identify the resources available, the obstacles that may be encountered. If there are a number of different paths to a goal, weigh up the benefits and disadvantages of each.

CHAPTER 6: EFFECTIVE IMPLEMENTATION OF GOALS

It's important to emphasize the importance of your client taking ownership of the entire process. It is the client who identifies what they want. It is the client who conceives the vision, commits to it, plans it and executes it. The coach supports the client. Supporting your client in implementing their goals is obviously crucial, for if the execution never happens, or is attempted half-heartedly or with inadequate resources all the labors will be for nothing.

After your client has conceived a plan. He has set himself goals. He has planned for them. The resources are there. The goals are practical, achievable, and achievable within a certain time frame. The challenge now is to work at his goals consistently, effectively, and on schedule. While most people are often enthusiastic about goals they are often not so thrilled about the means to achieve them. Say a person has passion for chemistry, but in order to gain a chemistry degree he or she needs to study mathematics, for which he has no zeal. How then can you encourage your clients to maintain enthusiasm, not only for the destination, but for the journey as well? You want them to be excited about, and to enjoy, the trip.

Have you ever undertaken a task which seemed rather tedious, but unexpectedly discovered that you derived energy from doing it? For instance, you're a student looking for extra income; you may have paid bills by gardening. It involves a lot of work including plenty of weeding – not a very exciting activity. But soon, you developed a sort of rhythm. In time the rhythm became almost automatic, which means you could think about other things. It has become so automatic that it you could do calculations and solve problems in your head while pulling weeds! When you sat down at your desk later, all you had to do was set your ideas down on paper.

Encourage your client to ask himself or herself the question: "How will the task I undertake enhance me? How will it elevate me, raise me to a higher plane? How will it augment my strengths? How does it relate to the things I love, the things I am passionate about? How does it bring out my talents? What opportunities does it create? How can I make it fun and enjoyable? Can I be more creative about how I take it on? For example, if I have to exercise, perhaps I can go for a jog in a forest I love. If I have to study for a history exam, and exercise, why not recite the names of the Founding Fathers while I'm doing press – ups?"

If you modify behaviors in this manner, and repeat them over a period of time they will become habits, and if you repeatedly approach tasks in a creative manner your thought patterns will change. You will find that the most successful people have learnt to think creatively about everything they set their minds to.

CHAPTER 7: THE COACH - BUILDING TRUST

For this chapter, you will look at the previously discussed principles again, but focusing on distinct skills the coach will need to apply these principles. You will see some strategies than can be used to build trust, to challenge ways of thinking, to clarify goals, plan, and execute those plans.

It is worth repeating that trust is the foundation of the coach-client relationship. If a coach cannot establish trust everything else he or she does will be futile. You are not only encouraging trust between yourself and your clients. You also want your clients to trust themselves, to have confidence in their ambitions and their potential. You also want your clients to be worthy repositories of trust. Their successes will depend upon the degree they can inspire loyalty – and keep that loyalty – in others, whether they are employees, employers, clients, family, service providers and other people they will encounter in their journeys.

Trust, is often ignored and usually plays second to self-interest. But trust is really the bedrock of a happy and stable society. Pretty much all of the ills in society can be traced to its absence. Countries are not governed well because politicians breach the trust of the citizens. Businesses often go to ruin because management betrays the loyalty of employees and other stakeholders. Wars start because nations cannot trust each other. Families split, the bond of trust to protect and nurture the natural environment is frequently broken, etc.

So what can you do as a coach to build trust? The first step is to assess character – not only your client's, but your own.

You will do well to spend time dwelling on your own trustworthiness. This may take some courage, and you may have to ask other people how your employees see you. Are you known for keeping confidences? Do your employees respect you? Do you honor the terms and conditions of their employment? Do you have a reputation for being fair and honest? Do you tend to uplift people rather than criticize them? Depending on the answers to your questions, prepare to possibly make a few changes in your own conduct.

Then it is important to assess the character of the person you are coaching. Allow him to do it himself. Remember what was said about active listening. Pay attention not only to what your client says, but to what he doesn't say as well. Observe body language, tone of voice and mannerisms. Ask them open-ended questions, such as: who do you trust? Why do you trust that person? Who do you distrust? Do you think you are a trustworthy person? Why? What kinds of relationships do you value and why? What do you expect from those relationships?

In time you will gain an idea of the kinds of things that motivate your client in relationships. You can then identify, together, possible fears, suspicions, doubts, anxieties the client has in himself and in others. You can then address these together. Remember, your tone is friendly and non-judgmental. The client should be doing the reflecting. You can suggest thoughts to him, but avoid telling him what he should be thinking and saying. And remember that the same kinds of questions you ask of your clients are the same kinds of questions you should be asking yourself.

CHAPTER 8: THE COACH - CHALLENGING THOUGHT PATTERNS

As mentioned, the way you think and act is governed by your beliefs. These beliefs are deeply rooted in your psyche. Positive beliefs about yourself and others produce positive behaviors. Negative beliefs engender negative behaviors. You will build up a picture of someone's beliefs by observation and prudent, noninvasive questioning. You want to identify belief patterns that limit personal potential.

Every person acts according to a number of assumptions, of which they are usually utterly unaware. A person who has no tolerance for failure may have been brought up in an environment that valued success above everything. Someone that brims with confidence may have been raised to believe in themselves and their accomplishments. An individual who finds it hard to trust anyone may have been horribly betrayed by someone close at some time in their past.

Assumptions that limit potential need to explored and challenged. Again, the client needs to do this, not you. Do not make judgments about your client. You can help them to identify their beliefs, again, by prudent questioning. If you recognize a pattern of thought, suggest that, and ask the client if they recognize it too. Why should they think in a certain way? How do these thoughts impact on their outlook on the world and themselves? What are the bases of these assumptions? Are they reasonable? What would they prefer to be the defining assumption upon which their thoughts and actions are based? What would alternate assumptions look like? What would they produce? Why couldn't this happen?

Encourage your client to prove these assumptions to themselves. Frequently people will say what they think others want to hear, and this may be for various reasons – weakness, perception of being pressured, ease, avoiding the real issues, or even boredom with the process. And remember, you are probably being perceived not just as a coach, but as the boss, so they may very well be seeking to please or appease you.

It may be useful to encourage the client to question you. Why are you asking these questions? Why do you attach importance to them?

These questions must be probing. If the client does not reflect upon his or her own thoughts, no progress can possibly be made. At the same time, be wise in asking these questions. Recognize when you may have touched upon something that elicits a strong reaction.

If you encounter strong resistance, pull back, but don't ignore what has happened. Come back to it later when the client is calmer, and better prepared to face it. That resistance may be the key to revealing the client's assumptions.

Remember, you are dealing with individuals. Each character is different, and so you must treat them differently. What may be elixir for one may be poison for another. Be patient. Do not rush your clients. If an athlete attempts a race without adequate training he will likely injure himself and be unable to run for a very long time. Your clients will progress at different speeds.

Also remember what was mentioned about trust. You are not only challenging your clients, but yourself as well. Examine your own thought patterns, your own assumptions about yourself and the world. You will express these in your coaching, aware of it or not. You will not want to limit your coaching by your own assumptions. Indeed you may very well benefit from a coach yourself.

CHAPTER 9: THE VISION

What does your client want? This may seem a simple enough question eliciting a simple enough answer. Many people would answer that they want a good job that they can enjoy and that makes a lot of money. They might like to buy a new car and a boat and take the family on nice holidays. In other words, they want the standard package.

Yet does any of this really drive a person? Does it speak to who he is, inflame the passion and inspire the mind? Certainly the adage "money can't buy happiness" is a cliché. Money is certainly usefulness in procuring a certain degree of contentment! Yet it is equally true that a purely material motivation cannot truly bring peace and energy to our lives.

Read about the lives of highly successful women and men, and you will find they all had something in common. They had a vision. They didn't simply have goals that they marked off a checklist as they achieved them. They energized their whole lives with one idea. That idea drove them and gave substance to their lives. Your client must discover his vision by realizing what empowers him, what drives him. What is his passion? And you, the coach, must help him. You can ask the client what they want to do. Not what they should do, or what is immediately practical, but what they want to do. Certainly, what they wish to do is going to be framed by what is achievable. But for now, you are helping the client to establish a vision for themselves. What would be their measure of a successful life? What contribution do they want to make to society and the world? What is it that would motivate them to get out of bed every morning? What would they want to be said about their lives when they are dead?

Considering relationships are very important in imagining a vision. Which relationships are important in their lives? What will they do to keep those relationships strong, especially when the significant people in their lives have life visions of their own? So many relationships break down because visions become obsessions rather than life giving, energizing perspectives. Such obsessions can isolate and blind people to the real needs and desires of others.

Suppose your client has envisaged a plan and motivation for that plan. In corporate terms it might be called a mission statement, a declaration of goals, actions to achieve those goals, and the values that infuse and animate them. Now you and the client must formulate strategies to implement that statement.

CHAPTER 10: THE STRATEGY

The journey is of course, just as important as the destination. Otherwise you would never arrive at the destination. Strategies to implement your client's vision must be clear, sound and sure. And here the hard work begins.

In developing strategies, the coach and client will need to consider a number of things. There is the objective, that is, the end to which subordinate goals are ordered. The objective of a client may be to conduct research in medicine that will enhance lives. However there will be a number of goals they need to achieve in order to get there – it may be to study, find a mentor, obtain a research grant, or any number of others.

Then there is planning. How is your client to achieve these goals? You will consider resources, both material and personal. Is your client capable of achieving the goals? If not, how can they be made so?

Finally there are values. What are the moral principles and standards of behavior that motivate the journey? How are these going to motivate, direct and stabilize the client on their way? What is the ethical framework of their enterprise? This is important, because this is what will give meaning to what they do.

These considerations give a broad context for framing a strategy. Then you can start asking specific questions to construct a specific strategy. You will need to ask the client who they think their clients/customers will be? What needs they have? What values, strengths and talents they can bring that possible competitors could not?

To maximize the chances of success, competition will have to be considered. What advantages could the client use and/or acquire? What competitive edge could they bring to their enterprise? How will they distinguish their service from competing ones? What investments could they make? What investments do they need to make to remain competitive? What will they do within the next few years to widen the gap over their competitors?

Then you will need to consider how the client's enterprise will make money. How much will they need to start? What is a viable revenue flow? How is that to be achieved? How will they maintain growth and profitability?

Even though these questions use the language of business, this sort of strategic planning applies to all sorts of enterprises. Non-profit enterprises and community projects still need to be conceived in terms of resource management and maximization. They must still be competitive, and profitable in the sense that something of value must be produced.

CHAPTER 11: GOALS

In the last chapter, you've set broad goals in the context of conceiving a vision for the client or the person you are coaching. Now, however, the goals need to be specified to align with the strategy. These will be the milestones by which you know that the strategy has succeeded. Goals motivate. They provide something concrete to drive individuals and teams. They are a reward for hard work.

A good coach will help the client set goals and always within the context of the original vision. They must be actionable and specific. The goal to "respond to customer complaints within 8 hours and resolve 90 per cent of them within 48 hours" is a much better goal than "respond to customer complaints as soon as possible." The first one is more actionable. In addition, it is measurable. You can easily determine if the goal is being achieved or not.

So goals should be specific, achievable, measurable and clear – that is, unambiguous and readily understood. Another important principle for defining goals is that there should only be a few goals set. What is easier and more manageable? Achieving one goal or ten? If someone tackles one goal at a time they are more likely to succeed. Whereas if they have ten, their time and energy will be spread over a wide area, and in all probability, none of the goals will be achieved within the given timeframe. It makes sense to assign an individual to work toward one key goal.

This key goal is the one overarching goal that defines the enterprise. People often set themselves up for failure because they give each goal equal value. They may decide that this year they will increase their writing output by 30%. They want to increase their income by 40%. They also want to finish restoring the roof, spend one day a week as curator of the local museum and attend six writing workshops. Clearly you need to prioritize your goals. Which one is the real priority? Which one really encapsulates what you want from my life right now? Given your desires and needs, which goals could be postponed, without necessarily abandoning them altogether? And so you must decide what is the primary goal of your client's enterprise.

In defining the key goal, ask yourself what the purpose of the enterprise is. Why does your client want to do it? What is the goal that will decide if it succeeds or fails? What goal posts could be shifted without emptying the entire project of its purpose and meaning?

Once you have your key strategic goal, you can set subordinate goals. Divide the enterprise according to its functions and assigns goals for each. You can then progress down the chain of responsibility, setting goals for teams and finally for individuals.

CHAPTER 12: FOLLOWING THROUGH

A great plan and a magnificent strategy is one thing. However, it will not amount to anything without hard, solid application. Many fantastic ideas fail because they are poorly executed.

There are several explanations for failures on implementing plans. If you're in a team, often a few individuals only know the strategic goals. If most of the members of the team don't know what they're doing then they can hardly be expected to implement the vision. The answer to this is to educate all of the team, and inform each group what their particular goal within the grand strategy is, and how that goal will contribute to ultimate success.

Even when the team knows what's going on, they may not know how they're scoring. Let them know. Provide benchmarks for them, achievement goals that will indicate how they're doing. Give them a sense of ownership and a sense of accountability. Give them feedback. Have regular meetings to assess progress. Often accountability is punitive, a put-down that is very often the first and only indication an employee has of the progress he or she is making. By that time intervention is too late. Constant, positive and encouraging interactions are much more productive.

Projects often fail in execution because the architect involves herself or himself in every level of the process. Every person has met bosses like this. They will not delegate. The danger is obvious. It is impossible to deal with everything, and given the volume of demand, attention will be focused on what is urgent, not what is important. Suppose you are building a house. The roof needs serious attention. The materials used have proved inadequate. The roofer has some ideas on what to do but can't talk to you because you are talking to the electrician about the light fittings. In the meantime the bathroom tiling needs to be attended to, and now, because the sale at the store ends next week. Then there's the decision about the nailing in the window frames. What size and quality should you use? Your time is engrossed with all these things, but which one is the more important? The roof, obviously.

If the plan has been well made there is a person at every level of the project in charge who knows their job. Let them do it. You should only make the most important decisions and on a macro level.

On an organizational level, the coach will help each manager in the project to also identify their most important goals and work toward them. The more these goals can be divided into steps the better. There will be goals for each year, another for each month, and another for the week. This way everyone knows what they are striving for at every level of the project, and they know where they are heading. It also makes the management of the whole project far easier.

The various members of the team will be easier to motivate, and indeed, more inclined to motivate themselves, if they can see the ultimate goal, where they are in achieving that goal, and where they need to be at any given stage in the project. They need benchmarks.

These benchmarks should be measurable, tangible and obviously achievable.

CHAPTER 13: ACCOUNTABILITY

Setting goals motivates individuals. Yet there must also be accountability. An individual may be less committed to achieving goals if they do not have a sense of responsibility for achieving those goals.

This is why setting meetings to monitor the progress of a project is so important. Team members can use meetings to assess where they are in terms of the project. They are opportunities to discuss what's going right and what's not. They celebrate achievement and assess failures to see how these failures can be overcome.

These are not naming and shaming sessions. This is completely unproductive. There is no blaming and there is no castigation from the project manager. Rather these meetings are for sharing and support. They should encourage and iron out any problems that individuals are experiencing. And very often, a problem experienced by one is experienced by many so complete honesty is required.

Too often group goals are jeopardized because of the absence of accountability. Often individual accountability is stressed to the detriment of group accountability. Accountability is often passed on from management and the team to the individual. Apart from being unfair this means that the team and its management never form a complete idea of what is happening. The risk then is that goals will not be achieved and the entire project will fail.

These regular meetings should be brief – half an hour at the most. It need only consider the most important goals. They should avoid minutiae, office politics, unimportant meeting procedures, philosophical arguments and chit-chat.

Managers should not dominate these meetings. It is a meeting of peers holding each other accountable and supporting each other.

If a member of the team is struggling to achieve a goal the rest of the team does not castigate him or her. Rather they work together to assess the problem and find a way to overcome it.

CHAPTER 14: FEEDBACK

Everyone likes to know how he or she is doing. While a pat on the back is nice, most would want to hear if they're not quite making the grade. They want to achieve. They want to succeed.

Not all feedback is good or useful. In fact the bulk of feedback people receive from peers tend to be negative, or otherwise not focused on strengths and abilities. People might hear a cursory "Well done. That was good," but that doesn't really say anything at all. Why was "it'" good? What was "it" anyway? What was the you're you were meant to have done well? If you don't know why it was well done how can you repeat the success?

But let's step back a moment. What is the purpose of feedback? Surely it is to help the recipient achieve their goals, drawing on their strengths, talents and abilities. From a manager's point of view it may be to make sure their project gets done. However, from the recipient's point of view there is a personal reward to be gained. They don't simply want that warm fuzzy feeling of being acknowledged. They want to know personal fulfillment.

They also want feedback that is eminently practical. They have all experienced honest but utterly useless comments.

Now who should be giving the feedback? Let's remind ourselves of the purpose of coaching. It is to unlock potential, allow the individual to see it and to achieve their goals. In this light it makes sense that the first person to be giving feedback should be the individuals concerned. It is they who should be asking themselves questions like:

- What did I do well?
- What could I have done better?
- How do I feel about what I have done?
- What would I have done differently?
- What have I learned?
- What have I discovered about myself?
- Where can this feedback take me if I act on it?

The role of the coach is to help them ask these questions to themselves. The coach can refine the questions and assist the individual to hit the target. If the client owns the questions they will also own the answers. They will become accountable.

Recall the best advice you ever received – advice that changed your life. Chances are you gave that advice to yourself. Someone may have been a sounding board for you. But they simply empowered you to realize what you truly wanted and liberated you to make a decision.

This is what coaches do. They liberate individuals to assess themselves and their desires without fear of judgment. Open the book and let your client read it. Then they'll give you their opinion. The best advice you can ever gave someone will not come from your own mouth. Instead it will come out of you listening to the client and confirming what you're hearing. You, essentially, speak the client's own thoughts back to them. This gives the client opportunity to reflect on what they themselves had said, and come to an objective assessment. Sure, you might need to help clients do that. You may need to tweak out the assessment a little bit, but your client is making the decisions. You are facilitating them to take ownership of the whole process.

Be aware too that what is good for the goose is good for the gander too. Prepare for some honest feedback on your own coaching and management skills. Receiving feedback will not make you appear weak. On the contrary you will appear as someone who practices what they preach. You will be someone who is constantly striving to learn. You will be leading by example. And you might just learn some things about yourself that you really do need to know.

Think of the coach as a sounding board. You are only reflecting what is said. You don't have to be an expert psychologist and problem solver. In fact the less powerful you appear in that respect the more effective the feedback is likely to be. Most people are often feel beholden to professionals to accept their advice, whether they entirely understand and accept it or not.

However, you do need to believe in the greatness that everyone possesses. There is power and drive in every person. It's just that many people haven't discovered it yet As mentioned before, there is nothing pretentious in this. You are making up nothing. You don't have to inflate egos and invent dreams. Every individual possesses strengths and abilities that can cause him or her to shine.

Remember though that you are also reflecting the truth. The individual you are coaching may discover some hard facts about themselves. Discovering greatness may entail uncovering weaknesses too and no one likes to face their weaknesses. Your role will be turning what may be a negative perception into a positive one. Reflection and openness will reveal insights that provide opportunities for change and growth. You will need to be supportive. An effective coach will create a safe space, free of judgment, within which the client can reflect.

A good coach will see their client through the good times and the bad times.

Be aware that some individuals may become emotional when considering feedback. Do not judge. Do not draw attention to the response. Give them time to settle and to reflect. You may want to say something like "perhaps we can leave this for now, and re-visit it later." It is important though that you do return to the issue when the client is feeling safe.

Never make a person the issue. Rather you are dealing with the issue itself. So, for example, if your client is presented with data that suggest that her targets are not being reached consistently, do not interrogate her as to why she is not achieving those goals. Rather ask her what she thinks the data might be suggesting.

CHAPTER 15: TALK

You will have noticed something of the style of coaching. Remember it isn't traditional authority-centered teaching but rather it focuses on individuals and their needs, desires and capabilities. You, as coach, aren't coming from a position of power. Rather you are showing the client the power they have.

Your language needs to reflect that. And it also needs to be able to address weakness and encourage improved performance in a positive manner. You need to be both respectful and honest. In your coaching, never speak in an accusatory fashion, forming judgments. Rather speak as an observer. Enable them to form their own judgments about their thinking and behavior.

For example, you might walk into the kitchen and say to my partner, "You didn't clean the dishes last night." You are addressing your partner, not what has happened. Instead you should say something like, "I see the dishes are dirty."

You can see that my partner has an opportunity to reflect on the state of the dishes and perhaps offer an explanation. And indeed there may be a very good explanation. However, when you place the focus on a person, such as your partner, you straight away put that person on the defensive and set up a potential conflict. You are no longer a coach but an authority or adversary.

Likewise if you need to make an observation or comment do not target the person. So don't say, "You didn't make your quota last month." Rather say, "I noticed that the quota wasn't filled last month." The difference may seem subtle, but it is there and it is important. In the first, you infer judgment about the person, or at least that is how the statement is received. In the second, you are presenting a situation and allowing the person to reflect on it. It may be that the person is experiencing an obstacle and you just might be able to help.

John Wooden was head coach of UCLA Bruins and won 10 National Collegiate Athletic Associate National Championships. You might think he would have had to have some pretty hard words with his team to achieve that kind of success. But he is quoted as saying; "A coach is someone who can give correction without causing resentment."

CHAPTER 16: COACH TO MAKE COACHERS

Great coaches will always be needed and you will always find clients. But a good coach's goal is to build up a team that will be autonomous. It will make its own good decisions, achieve its aims, self-monitor, assess, and be led by individuals who will be powerful and positive coaches themselves. Then you can move onto your next project!

The goal then is to establish not simply a team of individuals that will accomplish a set task, but a self-sustaining culture that will encourage innovation, creativity, goal setting, self-monitoring and self-assessment.

To assess how this culture is growing, you will need to ask yourself some questions.

- Are these people growing in their roles? Are they confident? Do they have ideas? Do they motivate others?

- Are you providing the opportunities, training and mentoring they need to grow in their roles?

- Is achievement being rewarded and celebrated?

If the team is producing excellent results with the minimum input from yourself you may be confident that you have an autonomous project or at least one that is well on the way to becoming so. Ask yourself, "If I were not here for six months would I be confident that the project would be on schedule for completion when I returned?"

CONCLUSION

Coaching is a privilege. A coach is in a position of trust. Individuals open their hearts to them. They expose their thoughts and desires to them. The coach should be humbled by that and perhaps even a little bit frightened.

It is certainly healthy to approach the task of mentoring someone with a little trepidation. It is good to be reminded of the preciousness and delicacy of the lives in your trust. And if you are aware of this, you are more likely to succeed.

You may have to challenge your own way of thinking. Perhaps you will have to re-assess your management style and the way you relate to your employees or clients. Embrace the challenge. Don't be afraid of it. Be open to discover your own power.

You will make some mistakes. Everyone makes mistakes, especially in new ventures. If you own mistakes to your coaching clients you will not lose their trust and respect. On the contrary, people are generally more apt to open themselves to individuals who own their fallibility than to those who admit to doing no wrong.

Being human is an absolute asset. The possibility of failure should not prevent you from striving to be more than what you are. After all, that is what you as coach are trying to impress upon your clients. As mentioned before, what is good for the goose is good for the gander.

The rewards are colossal. They are unknowable in fact. The changes you could make to the lives of others and your own are really immeasurable. Your actions will ripple down through generations in ways you cannot imagine. Did Einstein's math teacher realize that one of his pupils could be one of the greatest scientific minds of all time? Had Pierre de Coubertin's gym teacher any idea that the child he was coaching would become the father of the modern Olympic Games?

You may not coach a genius but you will be changing lives for the better and not the least your own. The qualities you cultivate and the skills you acquire not only make you a better manager but a better human being.

THANKS FOR READING

We really hope you enjoyed this book. If you found this material helpful feel free to share it with friends. You can also help others find it by leaving a review where you purchased the book. Your feedback will help us continue to write books you love.

The Smart Reads library is growing by the day! Make sure and check out the other wonderful books in our catalog. We would love to hear which books are your favorite.

Visit:
www.smartreads.co/freebooks
to receive Smart Reads books for FREE

Check us out on Instagram:
www.instagram.com/smart_readers
@smart_readers

Don't forget your 2 FREE audiobooks.
Use this link www.audibletrial.com/Travis to claim
your 2 FREE Books.

SMART READS ORIGINS

Smart Reads was born out of the desire to find the best information fast without having to wade through the sheer volume of fluff available online. Smart Reads combs through massive amounts of knowledge compiles the best into quick to read books on a variety of subjects.

We consider ourselves Smart Readers, not dummies. We know reading is smart. We're self taught. We like to learn a TON about a WIDE variety of topics. We have developed a love for books and we find intelligence attractive.

We found that each new topic we tried to learn about started with the challenge of finding the pieces of the puzzle that mattered most. It becomes a treasure hunt rather than an education.

Smart Reads wants to find the best of the best information for you. To condense it into a package that you can consume in an hour or less. So you can read more books about more topics in less time.

OUR MISSION

Smart Reads aims to accelerate the availability of useful information and will publish a high quality book on every major topic on amazon.

Smart Reads hopes to remove barriers to sharing by taking the copyright off everything we publish and donating it to the public domain. We hope other publishers and authors will follow our example.

Our goal is to donate $1,000,000 or more by 2020 to build over 2,000 schools by giving 5% of our net profit to Pencils of Promise.

We want to restore forests around the globe by planting a tree for every 10 physical books we sell and hope to plant over 100,000 trees by 2020.

Doesn't it feel good knowing that by educating yourself you are helping the world be a better place? We think so too...

Thanks for helping us help the world. You Smart Reader you...

Travis and the Smart Reads Team

WHY I STARTED SMART READS

Every time I wanted to learn about something new I'd have to buy 20 books on the topic and spend way too long sorting through them and reading them all until I arrived at the big picture. Until I had enough perspectives to know who was just guessing, who was uninformed and who had stumbled upon something remarkable.

I wished someone else could just go in and figure that out for me and tell me what matters. That's how smart reads was born. I want smart reads to be a company that does all that research up front. Sorts through all the content that is available on each topic and pulls out the most up to date complete understanding, then have people smarter than me package the best wisdom in an easy to understand way in the least amount of words possible.

For example, I got a new puppy so I wanted to learn about dog training. I bought 14 different books about dog training and by the time I got through the first 5 and finally started getting the big picture on the best way to train my puppy she had grown up into a dog.

Yeah she's well behaved. She doesn't poop in the house. I can get her to sit and come when I call. But what if someone else went in and read all those books for me, found the underlying themes and picked out the best information that would give me the big picture and get me right to the point. And I'd only have to read one book instead of 15.

That would be amazing. I would save time. And maybe my dog would be rolling over, cleaning up after my kids and doing the dishes by now. That my friend, is the reason I started smart reads. Because I wanted a company I can trust to deliver me the best information in an easy to understand way that I can digest in under an hour. Because dog training is one of many subjects I want to master.

The quicker I can learn a wide variety of topics the sooner that information can begin playing a role in shaping my future. And none of us knows how long that future will be. So why not do everything we can to make the best of it and consume a ton of knowledge. And I figured all the better if I can also make a positive difference in the world.

That's why we're also building schools, planting trees and challenging ideas about copyright's place in today's world. Because as a company we have to be doing everything we can to support the ecosystem that gives us all these beautiful places to read our books. Thanks for reading.

Travis

Customers Who Bought This
Customers Who Bought This Book
Also Bought

Unlocking Potential: Master the Laws of Leadership

Mastering Your Time: Learn How Successful People Enhance Productivity, Beat Procrastination and Do More in Less Time

Overcoming Procrastination: Proven Strategies on How To Improve Focus, Get Things Done and Achieve Your Goals

Reinvent Yourself: Become Instantly Likable, Captivate Anyone in Seconds and Always Know What To Say

Minimalism: Declutter, Organize and Reclaim your Space

Develop Self-Discipline: Daily Habit to Make Self Confidence and Will Power Automatic

Self-Esteem Supercharger: Build Self Worth and Find Your Inner Confidence

Success Principles: Techniques for Positive Thinking, Self Love and Developing a Powerful